Kev.

MW00937105

The Inspirational Story of Basketball Superstar Kevin Durant

presentation of the information is without contract or any type of guarantee assurance.

The trademarks that are used are without any consent, and the publication of the trademark is without permission or backing by the trademark owner. All trademarks and brands within this book are for clarifying purposes only and are owned by the owners themselves, not affiliated with this document.

Table Of Contents

Introduction

Chapter 1: Growing Up

Chapter 2: Early Basketball Career

Chapter 3: NBA

Chapter 4: Off the Court

Chapter 5: Charity and Legacy

Chapter 6: Notable Statistics and Awards

Conclusion

Introduction

As the title already implies, this is a short book about [The Inspirational Story of Basketball Superstar Kevin Durant] and how he rose from his life in a troubled area of Maryland to becoming one of today's leading and most-respected basketball players. In his rise to superstardom, Kevin Durant has inspired not only the youth, but fans of all ages throughout the world.

This book also portrays the struggles that Kevin Durant had to overcome during his early childhood years, his teen years, all the way up until he became what he is today. A notable source of inspiration is Durant's own foundation, which was named after him, as well as his consistent support of other charitable organizations, such as the Boys and Girls Foundation, the Red Cross, and numerous others. He continues to serve as a humble, mild-mannered superstar in a sport that glorifies flashy plays and mega personalities.

Thanks again for grabbing this book. Hopefully you can take some of the examples from Kevin's story and apply them to your own life!

Chapter 1:

Growing Up

Family

Kevin Wayne Durant was born on September 29th, 1988 in Washington, D.C. He was raised by his mother, Wanda Pratt, and his grandmother, Barbara Davis. He grew up with one sister, named Brianna, and two brothers, Anthony and Rayvonne.

His father, Wayne Pratt, left the family before Kevin's first birthday. Kevin had already reached the age of 13 years old when Wayne decided to come back into his life. Nonetheless, his parents were government employees. Wayne worked for the Library of Congress, while Wanda was a postal employee.

During his childhood, Kevin was teased by his schoolmates for always being the tallest in the class. This made him self-conscious about his height, so his mother had to ask his teachers to put him at the end of lines, in order for him not to stand out as much.

Growing up, Kevin was very close to his grandmother. Despite his feelings of insecurity regarding his height, she was convinced that his height was a blessing.

Among his siblings, Tony, who was three years older than Kevin, was the closest to him. They grew up together in Seat Pleasant, Maryland, and like any pair of siblings, they had their share of fights. One time, Kevin got so mad that he threw a boot at Tony. Kevin missed but shattered the glass cover of a light switch behind his older brother. Tony, who used to work at McDonald's while in high school, lent $10 to Kevin to have the switch fixed.

They both loved sports, particularly basketball, while they were growing up. The brothers were big fans of different sports teams in the Baltimore area. Surprisingly though, Kevin admitted that he grew up rooting for the Toronto Raptors and Vince Carter, in particular. He went on to say that he badly wanted to play for the Canadian franchise because of the exciting Carter and their strangely appealing jerseys.

Aside from showing their support for local sports teams, the brothers also joined a wide range of after-school sports at the local Boys and Girls Club. Oddly, even though they were close in age, they never played on the same team. One game in which Kevin participated in would prove to be one of the highlights of his young life. He was chosen to play in the Jordan Brand Classic, an All-Star game featuring the best and brightest high school senior ballers in the nation. Kevin shared MVP honors with Thaddeus Young in a game where he met Michael Jordan face-to-face.

While Kevin went on to enjoy NBA success, Tony's basketball path brought him to St. John's Military School in Kansas, the Junior College ranks, and to Towson University, a Division I mid-major school. While playing for the Tigers, the 6'7 245-pound Tony went to their practices on board his 2007 Dodge Charger, a gift from his younger brother. That's certainly a nice way to pay off a $10 debt. Tony also plays in The Goodman League where some of the best players from Washington D.C. lace up and strut their stuff.

A bevy of current and former NBA stars, college players, and street ball legends play in the popular league. Those who regularly spend their summer in the Goodman League include the younger Durant, Michael Beasley, Tywon

Lawson, Brandon Jennings, Jason "White Chocolate" Williams, Gilbert Arenas, Brian "2 Fast 2 Furious" Chase, Travon "Grim Leaper" Smith, and Hugh "Baby Shaq" Jones. Tony once scored 34 points to help his team win a game in the league.

Childhood

As a kid, Kevin's only dream was to conquer the court at Seat Pleasant Recreation. The center was a one-story, brown-brick building just across the Anacostia River in suburban Washington, D.C. During that time, all he wanted was to be the best in his neighborhood. He never imagined that his dream would later lead him to bigger awards and recognition.

Kevin doubted himself and didn't know if he was going to make the local team. But when all was said and done, he made the cut. His height became one of his advantages, just like his grandma had said.

He wore jersey number 24 for one year and, during that period, playing for the recreation center's youth league team was the only thing on his mind. This was until an unsuspected woman approached him one day after playing.

The woman said that he should switch to jersey number 23, because he played like Michael Jordan, the greatest basketball player of all-time. That brief conversation was the beginning of a bigger dream for young Kevin.

Kevin started watching NBA games, which completely changed his outlook. He was ten years old when he told his mother that he was dreaming to become a professional basketball player. Wanda gave him time to think about his decision. Yet, she still received the same affirmative answer the next day. Wanda promised him that she would do everything she could to help him achieve his goal.

Although Kevin was certain about what he wanted to be someday, he had no idea of the difficult road ahead. His skill development was entrusted by his mother to Taras "Stink" Brown, on the recommendation of a family friend. Brown, coach of the AAU team PG Jaguars, was a strict and authoritative neighborhood coach. During his training with Brown, Kevin became a practice junkie. They did duck walks, jumped rope, and performed shooting drills. He learned three moves: A pull-up jumper, a two-dribble jump shot, and a baseline drive.

During that time, Kevin spent a huge amount of time at the Seat Pleasant Recreation. Barbara had to bring him food every day, because the Recreation became his second home. Usually, his workouts took eight hours per day!

Later on, Durant started walking and jogging to a hill. It was known by local ballers as the Monster Hunt's Hill. His teammates used to sprint up and backpedal down, once or twice, as their training. However, Durant would usually not stop running until he was exhausted and out of breath, no matter how many rounds it took.

Chapter 2:

Early Basketball Career

Amateur Athletic Union

Kevin played Amateur Athletic Union (AAU) basketball with the PG Jaguars in Prince George's County, Maryland. He decided to wear number 35 on his jersey to honor Jaguars' assistant coach Charles "Big Chucky" Craig, who was murdered at the age of 35. Craig was the team's much-loved driver who used his own van to take the team to their games. He also helped Kevin develop his skills since he was 8 years old. Big Chucky and Coach Stink would serve as more than Kevin's coaches.

They would go out of their way to support Kevin and his teammates. KD affectionately recalls how Big Chucky would provide him with pocket money or buy him a meal when he couldn't afford one. He even sometimes stayed at the Craig home when his mother was away. Other players emulated Kevin. His brother Tony wore number 35 when he played for Towson, while teammate Chris Braswell sported the number at UNC-Charlotte. Braswell, who was close to Big Chucky, also listed Craig as his deceased father in his official bio.

The Jaguars won two national championships with Kevin as a member of the squad. Although he was only eleven years old during their first championship, he wowed the crowd when he scored 18 points during the second half of the final game.

During that time, Kevin played with another future NBA player: Michael Beasley. He and Michael became very close during this time. They would ride the bus to school together after Michael's mother dropped him off at Kevin's home every morning. The two talented friends formed the Jaguars' nucleus along with Braswell, another bluechip recruit. Kevin and Michael once thought of themselves as the Michael Jordan and Scottie Pippen of the team. The Toni Kukoc tag went to teammate Brice Plebani, who is now a lawyer.

In 2003, the team disbanded and Kevin transferred to play on the DC Blue Devils. One of his teammates on that team was Tywon "Ty" Lawson, who also became a professional basketball player in the NBA.

National Christian Academy

Kevin played for legendary coach Stu Vetter at the National Christian Academy during his first two years of high school. During Kevin's freshman year, the older teammates didn't seem to give the talented, but unproven youngster, enough touches during games. It was so frustrating for him that he even thought of quitting, but chose not to, because he didn't want to disappoint his mother. She worked hard every day and took on extra shifts at work in order to earn enough money for their family's expenses. Keeping his poise, Kevin stayed with the team and did his best to showcase his talent when he received opportunities.

During that time, he continued to follow Taras Brown's program, in order to maximize his skill-set. Kevin also grew to 6'8" after a five-inch growth spurt before his sophomore year. Finally, after earning the trust of his teammates during his sophomore season, Kevin's hard work seemed to be paying off. He was named the local Player of the Year by the Washington Post.

Oak Hill Academy

After his first two seasons at National Christian Academy, Kevin enrolled at Oak Hill Academy in Virginia, where he and former teammate Ty Lawson were reunited. Oak Hill was, and still is, a known basketball powerhouse, and was a great opportunity for Kevin to get national attention while helping a top program. He spent a year in the acclaimed school and posted an average of 19.6 points per game and 8.8 rebounds per game for the season. He was also voted Second Team All-American by Parade Magazine.

Montrose Christian School

For his final year of high school, Kevin played for Montrose Christian School in Rockville, Maryland. A school notable for producing top-notch basketball talent, which included Greivis Vasquez, Terrence Ross, Justin Anderson, and Linas Kleiza.

Kevin, who already stood at six feet and nine inches but weighed a little over 200 pounds by this time, managed to enhance his skill-set during his senior year. He improved his scoring average to 23.6 points, while also grabbing 10.9 rebounds per game. His brilliant performance solicited him a place in the 2006 McDonald's All-American Boys Game which showcased all of the top high school players in the nation.

Kevin shared the John R. Wooden MVP award with Chase Budinger after they led the West team to a victory over the East team, highlighted by Greg Oden, Thaddeus Young, Brandan Wright, Gerald Henderson, Jr., Mike Conley, Wayne Ellington, and Kevin's old pal, Ty Lawson. Kevin dropped 25 points and collared 5 rebounds to lead his team, which included fellow future NBAers Brook and Robin Lopez, Spencer Hawes, Darrell Arthur, D.J. Augustin, and Daequan Cook.

College

Kevin's excellent statistics during high school and his phenomenal performance in the McDonald's All-American Game captured the attention of major college basketball recruiters, who saw him as the second-highest rated high school prospect of 2006. The guy in front of him was Greg Oden. This marked the first and certainly not the only time that the big man nudged the lanky wingman to grab the top spot.

The scouting report on Kevin was that he was a player with the "lethal combination of length and a pure stroke with NBA range". Basketball experts saw Kevin as a great scorer who could put the ball on the floor and fake out defenders on the perimeter like a guard. The knock against Kevin was his lack of explosiveness. Many critics also posited that Kevin had a tendency to be a passive defender and rebounder.

Still, Kevin was high on the wish-list of each and every team in the nation. He was offered a scholarship by different colleges nationwide and was even prompted by his former teammate, Tywon Lawson, to join him at the University of

North Carolina. Aside from North Carolina, Kevin considered powerhouses Duke, Connecticut, Kentucky, Louisville, and Texas.

In the end, Kevin chose to enroll at the University of Texas, in Austin, to play for the Longhorns. Since his first year of high school, a man named Russell Springmann had been in contact with Kevin. A Maryland native, Springmann was a Longhorn assistant when he first spotted Kevin plying his wares at the War on the Shore, a basketball tournament in Delaware. Springmann was clearly a large influence in Kevin's decision to go to the University of Texas for basketball, which he made before his senior year of high school.

Russell and Kevin's friendship carried over to the Longhorn assistant's heirloom. While watching an NBA game featuring Kevin, Russell and his wife, Neissa, were discussing baby names. Russell thought that "Durant's a cool name" and Neiisa responded to the affirmative. And so, when they gave birth to a son, they knew what name to give him.

Former Longhorn and current NBA free agent Maurice Evans also had a hand in Kevin's decision to play in Texas. Evans, who was then playing for the Los Angeles Lakers, took Kevin under his wings. The two trained together whenever they could.

Despite being so young, Kevin was already a dominant player during his first year of college. He started in all 35 games he played in and also scored 20 points in his college debut against Alcorn State. In total, Kevin scored 20-plus points 30 times, and 30-plus points 11 times. He also posted four 37-point games en route to an average of 25.8 points per game, which was good enough to place fourth in the country. Kevin also recorded an average of 11.1 rebounds - fourth highest in the NCAA, and 1.3 assists per game. Despite only being a freshman, Kevin seemed to be at a much higher skill level than his collegiate peers.

Kevin was the unquestioned leader of the young University of Texas basketball team, coached by Rick Barnes. Aside from Kevin, the team was highlighted by fellow newcomers D.J. Augustin, Damion James, Justin Mason, and second year guard, A.J. Abrams. The team also had sophomore Connor Atchley and big man Dexter Pittman on the roster. Kevin wasn't only the best player on his team, he was also physically superior to the competition when it came to his athleticism and height. Those physical gifts still serve as advantages, even to this day.

With Kevin leading the way, the Longhorns placed third in the Big 12 Conference with a 12-4 win-loss record. Although they lost to perennial powerhouse Kansas Jayhawks in the Big 12 Championship game by two points, there was still no doubt that Kevin deserved the Big 12 Tournament's Most Valuable Player award. He posted a record-breaking total of 92 points during the tournament, including 37 in the championship game.

The Longhorns' overall record was 25-10, which placed them among the Top 20 nationally ranked teams and they received an invitation to the NCAA Tournament. The team was able to get to the second round of the NCAA Men's Basketball Championship after beating New Mexico State in the opening game. However, the Longhorns lost to the University of Southern California by a 19-point margin in the second round of the NCAA tournament, ending their Final Four dream.

Aside from the Big 12 Conference MVP, Kevin was named National Freshman of the Year. He was also the first freshman to receive the Oscar Robertson and the Adolph F. Rupp awards. He was selected to play for the U.S.A. National Team, as well.

After one year of playing for the University of Texas and completely dominating the competition, Kevin and his family decided it would be best to join the upcoming NBA Draft to pursue his dream of playing professional basketball in the NBA.

Chapter 3:

NBA

2007-2008

In the 2007 NBA Draft, Kevin was selected by the Seattle SuperSonics, and became the second overall pick behind Greg Oden - who was taken by the Portland Trailblazers.

Kevin's offensive play suited his new team and he quickly became a nightmare match-up for most opponents. In his first professional game, he recorded 18 points, 5 rebounds, and 3 steals. Before the end of the season, Kevin had recorded his first double-double in the NBA, with 42 points and 13 rebounds.

But even though he had the talent to shoot from anywhere on the floor, Kevin lacked some crucial defensive skills, especially against forwards who were either stronger or quicker than he was. Kevin worked hard to use his height and speed to improve his game defensively as the year progressed.

The SuperSonics won only 20 games by season's end, but Kevin's excellent performances were still recognized by the National Basketball Association. He received the Rookie of the Year award after averaging 20.3 points to become one of three teenagers, along with LeBron James and Carmelo Anthony, to record at least 20 points per game in a season. He also grabbed 4.4 rebounds, dished out 2.4 assists, and had 1 steal per game. Kevin also shot the ball fairly well, connecting on 43% of his field goal attempts and 87% of his free throws. It was clear to many around the league that Kevin had a bright future and was definitely a gifted player that could cause match-up problems each and every night.

2008-2009

After Kevin's first season, the Seattle SuperSonics franchise moved from Seattle, Washington to Oklahoma City, Oklahoma. The team became known as the Oklahoma City Thunder and their uniforms were switched from the iconic green and yellow to their new colors - blue, yellow, and orange.

Kevin and Jeff Green were joined by 4th overall pick Russell Westbrook, a young player that showed potential during his time with the UCLA Bruins. The Thunder management and coaching staff, led by manager Sam Presti and new coach Scott Brooks, who replaced P.J. Carlesimo, were hoping that Russell Westbrook could potentially develop into a decent player.

Despite the team playing in a new city and in front of a freshly excited fan base, the Thunder struggled to win, but they still managed to improve on their previous year's record. Kevin's performance was still impressive throughout the season; he averaged 25.3 points per game and improved his rebounding average from 4.4 to 6.5, as well. His defense was coming along thanks to his hard work in the off-season, perseverance, and 7 and ½ foot wingspan.

Though the Thunder won three more games than the last Sonics team, they still finished in the bottom third of the league. Even with an entertaining core of Durant, Green, Westbrook, and defensive dynamo Thabo Sefolosha, the Thunder were far from being an intimidating team. However, they were still very young, with their key players all under the age of 25. Kevin and the rest of the team believed they were on their way to building something special in their new home state.

It was around this time that Kevin would first be known as "Durantula", after NBA writers coined the nickname. Kevin was called "KD", as well as "Kid Clutch" for his clutch plays during crucial moments of the game, and "Slim Reaper" mainly for being deadly from anywhere on the court, coupled with his lanky frame.

2009-2010

In their second season, the Oklahoma City Thunder finally found their winning mix. They started it off by playing smart, solid basketball. By the second half of the season, the team had a nine-game winning streak. With the addition of third overall pick, James Harden, through the draft and the emergence of last year's 24th overall pick, Serge Ibaka, the Thunder began to develop an identity as a team that could play with a fast-paced offense *and* force many transition baskets, due to their speed.

Kevin continued to improve and became the youngest NBA scoring champion ever at 21 years and 197 days, with an average of 30.1 points per game. He also averaged more rebounds, with 7.6, while getting 2.8 assists, 1.3 steals, and 1 block per game. Kevin's dominant play also led him to his first All-NBA team and first All-Star selection.

As a team, the Thunder improved by leaps and bounds. They won 27 more games than the previous year, to reach the .500 mark for the first time since the 2004-05 season when the franchise was still playing in Seattle. Among their wins were a 28-point pounding of the Orlando Magic, the eventual Eastern Conference champs, and a 16-point win over superstar Kobe Bryant and the reigning NBA champion Los Angeles Lakers.

The Thunder were able to make the Western Conference playoffs but lost against the Lakers in six games. Kevin scored 24 points in his first playoff game. Despite getting knocked out in the first round, this was a huge step for the franchise, as well as for Kevin and Russell's confidence. Many respected figures around the league did not expect the Thunder to take such a large leap from the 2008-09 season to the 2009-10 season. At this point, it was looking like the Thunder had a bright a future ahead.

2010-2011

As the new season arrived, Kevin signed a five-year contract extension with the Thunder that was worth approximately $86 million. With the amount of production Kevin had given the franchise, it was a no-brainer from the Thunder's perspective.

Once again, he came through for his team. The Thunder earned the fourth seed in the Western Conference after winning a total of 55 games. Kevin averaged 27.7 points per game to win the scoring title for the second year in a row. He was proving to be a bonafide superstar at this point, and the pressure for team success was starting to build.

The Thunder won three of the first four games against the Nuggets in the playoffs. The first game of the series saw Kevin set a new career high for most points in a playoff game with 41. In Game 5, the Nuggets started strong, which made it hard for the Thunder to keep their composure and win the game. Fortunately for Oklahoma City, Kevin went berserk and led a late comeback by scoring 16 points in the fourth quarter. He again had a total of 41 points for the night and, most importantly, Oklahoma City advanced to the next round of the playoffs. Teammate Serge Ibaka almost made history by blocking nine shots during the game. The record, held by Mark Eaton, Hakeem Olajuwon, and Andrew Bynum, stands at ten.

In their second round match-up, upset-conscious Memphis Grizzlies did not give them an easy time. The eighth-seeded Grizzlies had just come from an impressive series win against top seeded San Antonio Spurs. The Thunder lost two of the first three games of the series. In Game 4, they were able to tie the series with a thrilling triple-overtime win. The Thunder won the next game, but they failed to close out the series in Game 6. Kevin had a terrible shooting night, which allowed Memphis to push the series to a seventh game. Being the star player of the team, the pressure was on Kevin. Fortunately for the Thunder, he ended the series with an astonishing 39-point performance, which he earned by attacking the rim, drawing fouls, and hitting all of his free throws. The Thunder won 105-90.

In the Western Conference Finals, Oklahoma City faced the Dallas Mavericks. The Thunder dropped the first game but won the second. However, Dirk Nowitzki and the Mavericks swept the next three games and the Thunder's season ended abruptly.

Many people around the league were again impressed that the Thunder had taken such a huge stride in their development. For most teams, getting to the Conference Finals with such a young, inexperienced group of players would be a dream come true. For the Thunder, they were still hungry, and weren't satisfied with the success of the season.

2011-2012

Due to the NBA Lockout, the regular season was shortened from the normal 82 games down to 66. Despite this, Kevin was still able to have an amazing year. He started the season scoring at least 30 points in the first four games. He was only the sixth player in NBA history to accomplish such a feat. Not only that, Kevin even recorded the first 50-point game of his career - he scored 51 points on February 12th, 2012 against the Denver Nuggets.

With his leadership, the Thunder won 47 games and advanced to the Western Conference playoffs as the second seed. Kevin ended the regular season with an average of 28 points per game, which gave him his third straight scoring title. He improved his rebound, assist, steal and block average, as well.

Kevin earned another All-Star nod, but this time along with his teammate Russell Westbrook. Even coach Brooks joined in on the fun and led the Western Conference squad to a win against Eastern counterpart Tom Thibodeau.

Oklahoma City avenged the previous year's playoff exit by defeating the Dallas Mavericks in the first round. They also barreled their way through the Los Angeles Lakers and San Antonio Spurs during the playoff run, to get all the way to the final round. Kevin scored 34 points in 48 minutes to help defeat the Spurs and battle the Miami Heat for the right to be called NBA champions.

However, the Thunder fell short to the Heat and were defeated in five games. In the series with the Heat, Kevin averaged 30.6 points per game and played great defense. Despite coming up short, he did not shy away from the challenge of competing against the best player in the world: LeBron James.

After losing to the Heat in the Finals, Kevin admitted to being very disappointed and promised to work hard in the off-season. Even though the Thunder lost, Kevin Durant was now a household name, just like Kobe Bryant and LeBron James. There was no doubt that Kevin was one of the all-around greatest players in the world after completing such a stellar year.

2012-2013

Before the new season started, Oklahoma City traded the defending Sixth Man of the Year, James "The Beard" Harden, to the Houston Rockets for Kevin Martin, Jeremy Lamb, two first round picks, and a second rounder. Cole Aldrich, Daequan Cook, and Lazar Hayward also went to the Rockets as part of the trade. With both parties failing to agree on an extension, the team had no other recourse but to trade Harden to avoid paying the luxury tax. It was a decision that sports analysts believed negatively affected the team's chances of winning the championship.

Despite what could have been perceived as a huge setback, Kevin and Russell took advantage of more opportunities, and proved that they could become the best duo in all of basketball. Even Harden improved dramatically after getting the chance to be his own man. In fact, he was in the running for the 2015 MVP award before Golden State's Stephen Curry shot his way into NBA immortality.

Despite losing Harden, the Thunder were able to lock-in Serge Ibaka for four more years. The defensive ace agreed to a $48 million extension that would keep him in a Thunder uniform until 2017. The team also drafted Perry Jones III from Baylor and signed free agent big men Hasheem Thabeet, a former number two pick, and Daniel Orton, along with guards Andy Rautins and DeAndre Liggins.

Even with all the changes in personnel, the Thunder were still able to improve from the previous season. Russell kept on improving while Kevin was his usual self. In an overtime victory against the Dallas Mavericks on January 18th, 2013, Kevin netted a career-high 52 points. But even with a scoring average of 28.1 points per game, he was not able to defend his scoring title, which he lost to Carmelo Anthony of the New York Knicks.

Nevertheless, Kevin posted a 51 percent shooting rate, a 41.6 percent three point shooting rate, and a 90.5 percent free throw shooting rate. The combination of these efficient numbers made him reach another career milestone. Kevin became the youngest player in NBA history to join the 50-40-90 club. This amazing milestone put him in the same group as one of his childhood idols, Larry Bird.

The Thunder won a total of 60 games during the regular season. The team advanced to the playoffs as the first seed in the Western Conference. Unfortunately, during the first series against the Rockets, led by their old pal Harden, Russell Westbrook suffered an injury when guard Patrick Beverley hit him during a rugged play resulting in a torn meniscus. This forced Westbrook to miss the remainder of the post-season.

Because of Westbrook's absence, Kevin needed to step up for the Thunder. Although most people realized that the Thunder had no real chance to get back to the Finals without their superstar point guard, Kevin did not show any signs of weakness. He continued to lead the team and stay optimistic, even though his team was at a huge disadvantage with only half of their duo remaining. He averaged a career-high 30.8 points per game throughout the playoffs.

Kevin showed a high level of leadership after the injury to Westbrook, and really let everything out on the court. He gave everything he had and did all the little things for his team. He was facilitating, rebounding, defending the other team's best players, and of course, scoring with ease. However, Oklahoma City was eliminated by the Memphis Grizzlies in the second round of the Playoffs, after a grueling series.

After the smoke cleared, Kevin was selected to the All-NBA First Team after he placed second to LeBron James in the MVP voting. He was also voted onto the Western Conference All-Star Team once again.

2013-2014

Kevin continued his offensive onslaught during the 2013-14 NBA season. During the month of January, Kevin scored at least 30 points for 12 consecutive games. He averaged a whopping 35.9 points during that period, which also saw him garner a career high of 54 points against Golden State. Kevin finished the season with a new career high in points scored, at 32 per game. He also averaged 7.4 rebounds, 5.5 assists, and 1.3 steals - while hitting half of his total shots hoisted. Because of these impressive numbers, Kevin won the season's Kia Most Valuable Player award over the likes of fellow superstars LeBron James and Blake Griffin.

Oklahoma City fared almost as well as the previous season with a record of 59-23. After getting coveted big man Steven Adams in the NBA Draft, the team re-signed veteran Derek Fisher who eventually retired after the season. However, they lost Kevin Martin via sign-and-trade to Minnesota after his contract expired. Westbrook played only 46 total games, but still averaged more than 21 points. While he was out, Reggie Jackson was a big revelation - as he took over the reins and averaged double digits with 13.1 points per game to go with 4.1 assists and 3.9 rebounds. Serge Ibaka continued his surge as he averaged 15.1 points, 8.8 rebounds, and 2.7 blocks - up from the previous year's averages of 13.2 points and 7.7 rebounds. Kevin and the Thunder's core continued to get ample support from reserves Nick Collison, Caron Butler, and Jeremy Lamb, among others.

After getting the second seed in the Western Conference, the Thunder faced the Memphis Grizzlies in the first round. This marked the third time the two teams faced each other in the playoffs. With the Grizzlies coming out victorious the previous year, OKC was bent on exacting revenge. But things didn't pan out at first. Kevin would struggle with his rhythm during the first five games, which resulted in *The Oklahoman* calling him "Mr. Unreliable".

With the Thunder behind 2-3, Kevin rallied his teammates to take Game 6. He scored 36 points to silence his critics. The Thunder eventually won the next game and pushed past the Grizzlies into the second round. The first round series between Memphis and OKC is known for the four consecutive games that went into overtime, a league record. The Thunder went on to defeat the Los Angeles Clippers in six games, but lost to the veteran-laden San Antonio Spurs, 4-2, in the Western Conference Finals.

2014-2015

For Kevin, the 2014-15 NBA season was the complete opposite of the past year's MVP run. For the first time in his career, he suffered a major injury - which caused him to miss most of the season. A Jones fracture in his right foot sidelined him for the first 17 games of the season. He came back on December 2nd, but injured his ankle a few weeks later. He had minor surgery on his foot in February and was finally ruled out for the season a month later. All in all, Kevin played in only 27 games, in which he averaged a measly (by his standards) 25.4 points per game.

Like in the previous season, the Thunder lost a key part of their rotation via free agency. Defensive specialist and long-time Thunder guard Thabo Sefolosha's contract expired and instead of re-signing, he went to the Atlanta Hawks in a sign-and-trade deal. OKC made up for this by signing three-point specialist Anthony Morrow and journeyman point guard Sebastian Telfair. The Thunder also drafted Michigan's Mitch McGary and Stanford's Josh Huestis.

They later traded for Dion Waiters to strengthen the shooting guard position.

Oklahoma City finished with a 45-37 record, which was not enough to make the playoffs in the cutthroat Western Conference. However, not all was lost on the season. Because of Kevin's absence, Russell Westbrook was forced to grow as a player and as a leader. He rose to the occasion and enjoyed a breakout season while Kevin cheered him on from the sidelines.

From an impressive 21.8 points per game average in 2014, Westbrook exploded his average to 28.1. He also dished out 8.6 assists and grabbed 7.3 rebounds per game. Perhaps more than just statistically, Westbrook developed a reputation as one of the truly elite players in the entire league. Oklahoma City now had two of the best players on their team.

2015-2016

Long-time head coach Scott Brooks was fired in April of 2015 and was replaced by Billy Donovan, formerly of the Florida Gators. Kevin played for Brooks since the 2007-08 season when Scott was still an assistant coach to P.J. Carlesimo. Brooks was named interim coach after Carlesimo's firing and was promoted to Head Coach the following year, when the Seattle Supersonics moved to Oklahoma City.

Since then, Kevin and Scott, along with Russell and later Serge, grew together and enjoyed seven mostly successful seasons together, though they always fell short in their minds. The firing of the former Coach of the Year awardee was tough for Kevin, but he stressed that he supported the decision of OKC management.

As of this publication, Kevin is still feeling his way into basketball shape, as he has played in only 12 of the 19 games. However, he has averaged 28.4 points and 7.4 rebounds in over 35 minutes of playing time. His fellow superstar, Westbrook, is right next to him with 27.5 points, 7.3 rebounds, and 9.6 assists per game. Ibaka,

Kanter, and Waiters are all averaging double digits in points while The Big Kiwi, Steven Adams, has been starting for them. Only time will tell if this group will respond well to Donovan but from the looks of it, they may have a chance to go all the way.

Another source of joy for Kevin this season is his reunion with University of Texas teammate D.J. Augustin. Oklahoma got the services of Augustin after trading away Reggie Jackson, Kendrick Perkins, Grant Jerrett, Tibor Pleiss, and a first-round draft pick. Aside from Augustin, OKC got center Enes Kanter and shooter Steve Novak from the Utah Jazz, along with Kyle Singler and a second round draft pick from the Detroit Pistons.

The current season will be the last year of Kevin's $89 million, five-year contract. Surely, things will go ballistic once the season ends, media-wise. Aside from OKC, the teams that are strongly rumored to be interested in the services of one of today's brightest stars are the Los Angeles Lakers, New York Knicks, and Miami Heat.

Washington management and fans have started making recruitment pitches to Kevin. During his lone trip to his hometown to battle the Washington Wizards, the jumbo-tron showed a clip headlined "Come Home KD" with Kevin in his OKC jersey but with the word "Washington" photoshopped over it. Fans also carried signs saying "KD2DC". Though Kevin went on record to say the move was disrespectful, he will always have Washington in his heart. Whether "Washington" will also be in front of his jersey next year won't change the fact that Kevin is a loyal guy.

Chapter 4:

Off the Court

Endorsements

After being drafted into the NBA, Kevin has accumulated considerable means, not only through his professional playing career, but through numerous endorsements as well. As a matter of fact, Kevin is one of the top earning players in the entire NBA when it comes to endorsement deals. He has the most endorsement deals in the league.

The Thunder forward signed a seven-year contract with Nike, back in 2007, worth around $60 million. He chose Nike over Adidas, which offered him more - with a $70 million deal, simply because he had been wearing Nikes since he started playing as a kid. After the contract ended, Nike upped the ante by signing Kevin to a record-breaking 10-year, $300 million shoe deal.

Last year, Kevin signed a deal with Sonic, a fast-food chain popular for its drive-in restaurants. Sonic has around 3,500 branches all over the country but is based in Oklahoma. Kevin is the first endorser of the chain that comes from the sports world. Sparkling Ice, a brand of sparkling water with zero calories, is another company that teamed up with Kevin as it's first ever athlete endorser. Orange Leaf, a business that deals with low fat yogurt, is another Oklahoma-based franchise that Kevin endorses. Kevin is also earning his keep endorsing Kind, a nut and fruit bar brand.

In 2013, Kevin added Degree for Men and BBVA to his endorsement portfolio. In the same year, he became the fourth highest-earning basketball player, by earning $35 million. This year, Kevin ranks second to only LeBron James as the top earner. King James earned $64.6 million this season while Kevin has amassed $54 million.

Other endorsements that Kevin has, include the Oklahoma Department of Health, Skullcandy headphones, Neff, Sprint, Gatorade, Panini, and General Electric. He also appeared on a cover for

2K Sports. Kevin's move to Jay Z's Roc Nation in 2013 has already paid dividends, as he moved from fourth to second in the top earners list.

Film

Alongside Taylor Gray, Brandon T. Jackson, Doc Shaw, and Jim Belushi, Kevin starred in an international movie entitled "Thunderstruck". It was his first time to appear in a major motion picture.

At first, he turned down the offer because he didn't want to be involved in that type of project. Later on, however, he realized that the movie could serve as an inspiration to younger generations. The movie was directed by John Whitesell and was released on August 24th, 2012. With his role in the film, Kevin became one of the few successful athletes to star in a movie.

Kevin also appeared in the commercial "Back for the Future". Frank Marshall directed this Nike Air Mag commercial, which stars Christopher Lloyd as Doc Brown, Bill Hader, Tinker Hatfield, along with Kevin.

Music

Aside from playing basketball, Kevin has had a passion for hip hop music ever since he was a young kid. It was reported that he collaborated with another NBA player-turned-hip-hop-hobbyist by the name of Stephen Jackson, of the San Antonio Spurs. Kevin was working with him on the song entitled "Lonely at the Top" from Jackson's mix-tape, *Jack of All Trades*.

Meanwhile, among his hardcore fans, Kevin was already known by his rap name, Sniper Jones. He wrote a song entitled "Tha Formula", which is about the formula of success. Kevin gets help with the song from B-Simp. Kevin has also released "Worried Bout Tomorrow", "Wired/Paid In Full" and "Rolls Royce", which features Privaledge.

The music lover in Kevin has led him not only to make his own music, but to also guide young people through P'Tones Records, a non-profit after-school music program held across the nation. Kevin is the spokesperson of the non-profit organization's branch in Washington, D.C.

Chapter 5:

Charity and Legacy

Seat Pleasant Activity Center

Seat Pleasant Activity Center was basically Kevin's second home while he was growing up. It was the place that helped him to achieve his NBA dream. He put in so many hours of work in that building, and it helped to develop his character as well.

Now that he has become a basketball superstar, he goes back to Prince George's County to help the youngsters reach for their dreams. He made the recreational center a cool hangout for the youth by donating $25,000. The funds were used to renovate a gaming room, which was re-named "Durant's Den" as a tribute. The room has a vinyl floor that looks like a basketball court, lounge chairs and couches, bar stools, a PlayStation 3, an Xbox 360, a projection screen, and two 55-inch LCD flat-screen televisions.

Kevin Durant Charity Foundation

Kevin, sometimes known in NBA circles as "the nicest guy around" proves this label by continuously giving back to the community. He established the Kevin Durant Charity Foundation, or KDCF, to provide help to at-risk youth belonging to low-income backgrounds. Among the facets of their lives that the KDCF wants to improve, are education, youth development, health and wellness, fitness, and homelessness.

The foundation aims to help through various programs such as the "Build It And They Will Ball" project. This program aims to build and renovate basketball courts so that less privileged youngsters can have access to sports, particularly basketball. The project, which was introduced in 2015, will build courts across the United States and in other countries as well. The opening of the first U.S. court renovation was held in October 2015 at North Highland Elementary School in Oklahoma.

Another future endeavor of Kevin and his foundation is the Kevin Durant Transitional

House. The project is aimed at solving the problem of homelessness, especially among the young people of Prince George's County.

Kevin Durant Family Foundation

With the help of his mother, Kevin has launched a charity, which he named the Kevin Durant Family Foundation, in 2012. He chose to focus on the very things that have led him to where he is now: his mother's undying support, and the opportunity to be involved in recreational activities. Thus, he established programs not only for childhood education, but also for single mothers. The vision of the KDFF is to "play it forward" and to achieve it, the foundation raises money to support different programs.

Charitable and gift giving activities during the holiday season are part of Kevin's program as well. He's named it "Kevin's Christmas". The KDFF partners with the All-American City Grade Level Reading Award. It's main goal is to assist disadvantaged children so that they have the opportunity to become successful students.

Tornado Relief

Through the Kevin Durant Family Foundation, Kevin donated $1 million to the American Red Cross for relief, after tornadoes swept entire neighborhoods and killed at least twenty-four individuals in the Oklahoma City suburb of Moore, Oklahoma.

Kevin did not purposely try to announce his charitable act. It was Red Cross that broke the story on Twitter. Since the Seattle SuperSonics relocated to Oklahoma City, Kevin has considered it his home. He always makes it a point to show support to the fans of the team and to the community as a whole. Likewise, Kevin is highly regarded by the entire state of Oklahoma. He is embraced as a superstar on the court and a superhero who is humble and generous off of it.

Prince George's County

Once again, Kevin went back to his hometown in July 2013 for another charitable act. But this time, he shared his blessing to not just one, but three different organizations.

Kevin, through the Kevin Durant Family Foundation, awarded $150,000 to the Seat Pleasant Activity Center, the Maryland Jaguars Youth Organization, and the Community Kinship Coalition Incorporated. The funds would be used to enrich the lives of at-risk children, ages 6-28, through athletic, educational, and social program support. The foundation selected the said organizations because they were pivotal in Kevin's success.

All of these amazing acts of charity show Kevin's true character, and it proves that he has not forgotten where he's come from. Many times, famous celebrities lose the connection they had with the reasons they achieved their successes in the first place. Not Kevin. He remains humble and grounded, even through all of the million dollar contracts and ridiculous amounts of media attention.

These character traits are actually what makes Kevin so likable and why so many of the youth of today seem to relate to him. He doesn't talk or act much different than he did when he was a high school or college student, in terms of how he treats others. Many people have said, after meeting him, that they were surprised at how genuinely nice and caring he seems, even though they might be just another fan. It is a lesson we can all take and apply to our own lives.

Chapter 6:

Notable Statistics and Awards

College

Naismith National College Player of the Year (2007)

Consensus First Team All-American (2007)

NABC Division I Player of the Year (2007)

USBWA National Freshman of the Year (2007)

First freshman to earn the Big 12 Conference Player of the Year (2007)

Big 12 All-Defensive Team (2007)

Big 12 All-Rookie team (2007)

Oscar Robertson Trophy (2007)

Adolph Rupp Trophy (2007)

Led the University of Texas Longhorns to a 25-10 record and to the Second Round of the NCAA Tournament

First freshman to be named the National Player of the Year in NCAA history

First freshman to win the 2007 John R. Wooden Award

Ranked top four nationally in both scoring and rebounding, which made him the only player to be in the top list in both categories

First player in Big 12 history to score 400 points and grab 200 rebounds in conference play

Scored 30 points in nine games

Number 35 retired by the University of Texas

NBA Awards

NBA Most Valuable Player (2014)

Named to the All-NBA First Team five times (2010-2014)

Received the NBA Rookie of the Year award (2008)

Named the NBA Rookie of the Month five times (2008)

Named to the NBA All-Rookie First Team (2008)

Selected as an NBA All-Star six times (2010, 2011, 2012, 2013, 2014 and 2015)

Named the All-Star Game M.V.P. (2012)

Selected as the NBA Rookie Challenge MVP (2009)

Won the NBA All-Star Weekend H-O-R-S-E Competition (2009)

NBA Scoring Champion four times (2010-12, 2014)

NBA Milestones

Fourth player in NBA history to score at least 400 points during the first 15 games of a season at an age of 21 or younger (2009)

Set a new record in the Rookie Challenge after scoring 46 points (2009)

Second youngest NBA player to score 4000 points (2009)

Scored 30 points or more in seven consecutive games (2009-10)

8th player in NBA history to win three consecutive scoring titles (2010-12)

Youngest player to get the highest scoring average in a season, with an average of 30.1 points per game (2011-12)

International Career

Team USA

Kevin was invited to the training camp for Team U.S.A. in February of 2007. He was the second college freshman to be part of the training camp. The first one was Greg Oden, who also happened to become the first overall pick in the 2007 NBA Draft, ahead of Kevin.

Kevin only played in a couple of games in the 2007 NBA Summer League, but was still chosen to be part of Team U.S.A. He joined the State Farm U.S.A. basketball challenge with other NBA All-Stars including Kobe Bryant, Dwight Howard, Chris Bosh, and LeBron James. Yet, even with his impressive talent, Kevin did not make the final cut because he did not have enough experience relative to the twelve players left on the team.

Kevin finally got his chance to represent his country when he was chosen to be part of the team bound for the 2010 FIBA World Championship. Because some of the older players were not able to join the team, Kevin took on an important leadership role, as he was deemed the best of the lot. He was named the Team Captain and led them to a gold medal finish (the first in the event since 1994), while winning Most Valuable Player honors along the way.

He averaged 22.8 points, 6.1 rebounds, 3.1 assists and 1.4 steals during the tournament. He posted 28 points in the Gold Medal game against the Turkish national team. In total, Kevin broke the record of most points in the history of the tournament - with 205.

He also was a big factor in U.S.A.'s gold medal finish in the 2012 Olympic Games in London, England. Kevin averaged a team-high 19.5 points per game, including a 30 point outburst in the final game. He also grabbed 5.8 rebounds and had 2.6 assists and 1.6 steals each game, on a team that was absolutely star-studded.

Conclusion

I hope this book was able to help you gain inspiration from the life of Kevin Durant, one of the best players currently playing in the National Basketball Association.

The rise and fall of a star is often the cause for much wonder, but most stars have an expiration date. In basketball, once a star player reaches his mid- to late-thirties, it is often time to contemplate retirement. What will be left in people's minds about that fading star? In Kevin's case, people will remember how he led a franchise in their journey towards the championship. He will be remembered as the guy who plucked his franchise from obscurity, helped them build their image, and honed his own image along the way.

Kevin wasn't always the first choice while growing up, or in the draft, for that matter. He didn't always succeed in his early years, and struggled to get playing time during his early high school days. But as soon as he got his opportunities, he worked hard to maintain his standing and to reach the top.

Kevin has also inspired so many people because he is the star who never failed to look back. He's the one who paid his dues forward, by helping thousands of less-fortunate youth find their inner light through sports, specifically basketball.

Another thing that stands out about Kevin's story is the fact that he never forgot where he came from. As soon as he had the capacity to give back, he poured what he had straight back to those who needed it, and he continues to do so to this day.

Made in the USA
Middletown, DE
20 March 2018